TUDOR
1485–1603

STUART
1603–171...

VICTORIAN
1837–1901

MODERN TIMES
1901–NOW

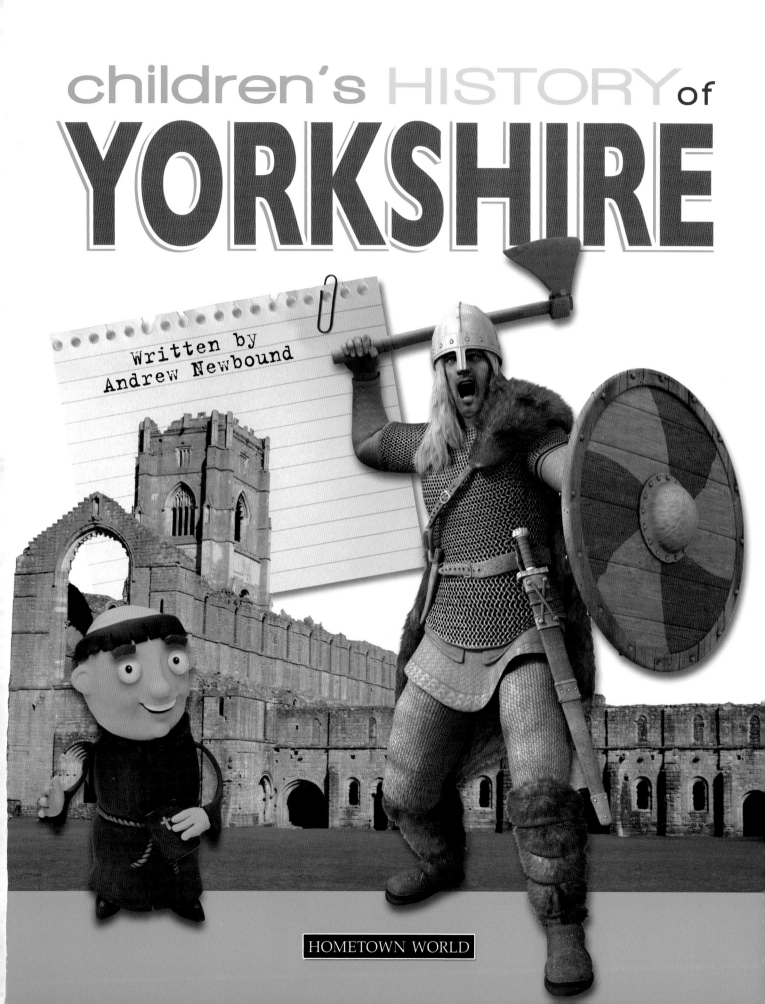

children's HISTORY of
YORKSHIRE

Written by
Andrew Newbound

HOMETOWN WORLD

How well do you know Yorkshire?

Have you ever wondered what it would have been like living in Yorkshire when William the Conqueror's army struck? What about working in the woollen mills? This book will uncover the important and exciting things that happened in towns and villages near you.

Want to hear the other good bits? Some rather brainy folk have worked on this book to make sure it's fun and informative. So what are you waiting for? Peel back the pages and be amazed at Yorkshire's very own story.

Timeline shows which period (dates and people) each spread is talking about

THE FACTS

'Spot this!' game with hints on something to find in the area

Fun facts to amaze you!

THE EVIDENCE

An imaginary account of what it was like for children growing up in Yorkshire

Intriguing photos

A summary explaining how we know about the past

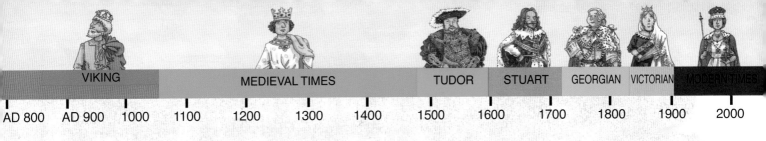

Contents

A Roman Message!

Vitus has been out gathering firewood for his tribe, the Brigantes. It's hard work, especially now in winter when icy rain lashes his face and cruel winds chill his hands. Today, though, he has more than the weather to fear. The Roman army has arrived and a Centurion has given him a message for his elders at Aldbrough: 'Yield or die!'

ROMAN BRITAIN AD 237

KEY
— road
fort major fort
▬▬▬ wall
Roman provinces

Hadrian's Wall
Ermine Street
BRIGANTES
Eboracum

The Romans Arrive

The Celtic tribe of Brigantes ruled Yorkshire from 500 BC. However, in AD 43 rumours began spreading from the south – a huge foreign army had invaded England! But it wasn't until AD 50 that the Romans' legendary Ninth Legion arrived in Yorkshire.

Most expected a huge and bloody battle but, instead of fighting, the Romans simply set up camp and lived peacefully with their Brigantes neighbours until AD 69. All that changed when the Brigantes civil war broke out. The Romans stepped in, defeated both sides and promptly took over Yorkshire.

The Romans set up camps all over Yorkshire. They built a network of straight paved roads that linked the forts, many of which are still used today.

The major Roman settlement in Yorkshire was Eboracum, which we call York today. Other settlements were also in places we know and live in today, such as Doncaster, Tadcaster, Boroughbridge, Malton, Ilkley, Catterick, Scarborough and Castleford.

New towns

Roman settlements and buildings were much better than the Brigantes' wooden forts. They introduced stone-built temples, baths, shops and markets. We also have the Romans to thank for sewers – Yorkshire must have been pretty stinky before they arrived.

KEY
- Barracks and other buildings
- Bathhouse
- Officer's house and headquarters
- Granary
- Workshops
- Gate
- Ditch and rampart

Lagentium Fort's North Gate

This plan shows what the Roman fort at Castleford may have looked like.

FUN FACT
A Roman mile was equal to 1,000 paces – about 1,480 metres.

Some of us Romans married Celts and settled down.

SPOT THIS!
You can still walk on the original Roman road on Wheeldale Moor on the North Yorkshire Moors.

Claudius is a Roman boy living in Britain. He is nine years old – the same age as Vitus. But their lives are very different. Here is an imaginary entry in Claudius's diary.

FUN FACT
Over a century ago, a local Castleford man dug up a complete Roman milestone dated AD 249. See it for yourself in the Leeds Museum.

We're not all from Rome. Some of us soldiers come from other parts of Europe!

Lagentium AD 138

Father says we're staying in Lagentium. I'd rather have stayed in Eboracum. This place is much smaller, and colder too. The locals call it Castleford, after the fort our soldiers built beside the river I suppose. Father says he can earn a good living here. He makes leather goods for the soldiers, like shoes, saddles, tents and shield covers. Lots of people pass through here on the road from Dunam (Doncaster) to Eboracum so we can sell a lot of his wares to these travellers. Some Brigantes locals are unfriendly, but I met a boy of my age called Vitus. He's quite nice. He lives in the vicus beside our fort. I can't believe that he doesn't have glass windows, central heating or even a sewer at his house. They are such savages!

Roman pottery found at Castleford has been carefully repaired.

This leather sandal belonged to a Roman soldier. The sole is studded with nails to make it last.

How do we know?

The 16th century historian William Camden was the first person to identify Castleford officially as the Roman settlement Lagentium, a claim people really started to believe when lots of Roman coins were dug up near the river.

In 1724, English archaeologist William Stukeley investigated Castleford further. He found the remains of Roman buildings and evidence of up to three separately constructed forts.

The Romans ruled Yorkshire for 400 years.

More recent investigations have uncovered more of Castleford's Roman past, including jars, handmade tiles, leather shoes and tents, jewellery, and even a pair of tweezers. A leather saddle cover helped specialists make a copy of the original. And a leather shield cover is the only find of its kind from anywhere in the Roman Empire. Perhaps most exciting of all was the discovery of stone foundations belonging to a stable block, barracks and a well-preserved military bathhouse.

CELT
500 BC

ROMAN
AD 43–410

ANGLO-
SAXON
AD 450–
1066

VIKING
AD 865–
1066

MEDIEVA[
TIMES
1066–148

New Kingdoms

Edwin sits wounded on the battlefield, his leg torn by the blade of an enemy sword. All around him the clang of metal rings out; men shout and scream as the army of Yorkshire fights to repel invading Angles from Germany. Edwin's men have fought hard but this battle is lost. The Angles are bigger and stronger – and here to stay!

Map of Angle-Land AD 600–900

This map shows the Anglo-Saxon Kingdoms in AD 600–900.

Anglo-Saxons

When the Romans left Britain, new invaders arrived. In AD 560, warriors from what is now Germany sailed up the Humber and decided to stay. They were the Angles and the Saxons. They were taller and more muscular than the Yorkshire folk who were around at the time, which probably helped when it came to fighting over land. So it'll be no surprise to learn that the Angles, led by their king, Aelia, quickly took control of most of Yorkshire, which they called Deira.

Despite being smaller and weaker, not all Yorkshire folk gave in to the Angles. In Celtic areas, known back then as Craven, Elmet and Loidis, men fought back and managed to stay independent for a number of decades. Today, we know these areas as West and South Yorkshire, with Loidis being near Leeds.

8

...AD 560 ANGLES INVADE...AD 604 BERNICIA AND DEIRA UNITED...

Cruel Times

These were violent times. The Yorkshire we know today was split into four independent kingdoms – the Angles of Deira and the Celts of Craven, Elmet and Loidis. Each had its own king and if they weren't fighting each other, they were battling it out with Northumbrian armies from the north, or Saxon armies from the south. Eventually, the three independent Celtic Kingdoms were defeated by King Edwin of Northumbria in AD 617.

Skeletons of Anglo-Saxons aged from 18 to 45 dug up at Walkington Wold.

FUN FACT
Anglo-Saxons were known to behead criminals, then display the heads on spikes as a warning to others.

Angles and Saxons together are called the Anglo-Saxons.

How do we know?

Tor Dyke, stretching between Upper Wharfedale and Coverdale, was an Anglo-Saxon defence. You can still walk the two-kilometre-long wall. Archaeological excavations, have helped us piece together bits about Anglo-Saxon life. Thirteen headless bodies were found in an area known locally as Hell's Gate. A famous Anglo-Saxon helmet was found in May of 1982 as builders dug the foundations for a brand new shopping centre in York. Was your town once an Anglo-Saxon settlement? See if the name of your town or village includes any of these Saxon words!

SAXON PLACE NAMES

dun = hill
eccles = church
ham = farm
ley = clearing
straet = street
tun or ton = village

Viking Trade

Eric hardly ever thinks of his Scandinavian home. He's far too busy working in the bustling Jorvik markets where Viking traders like him sell their wares. The smell of fresh leather wafts across from the shoemakers opposite, pigs grunt and squeal in pens nearby, and eager locals queue to buy Eric's pots, pans and fine metal jewellery. Times are good!

Jorvik means Horse Bay.

The Vikings

The year AD 866 was a bad year for the Anglo-Saxons. The ferocious Vikings first arrived led by their ruler, Ivar the Boneless. They sailed up the River Ouse and took over the Anglo-Saxon capital of York for a time. Later, in AD 869, they returned and this time stayed for an entire year. They must have liked it too, because by AD 876 they had settled for good.

The original wave of Viking invaders was young noblemen and their followers from Scandinavia. They found good farm land. Under their ruler Haden, the first Vikings settled in York – renaming it Jorvik – and made Yorkshire their home. Later settlers were ordinary farmers, traders and craftsmen who brought their skills and wares to Yorkshire.

...AD 876 VIKINGS SETTLE AT JORVIK...AD 954 ERIC BLOODAXE MURDERED...

VIKING PLACE NAMES

by = village
fell = hill
gat = road or way
kirk = church
thorpe = farm
thwaite = clearing

FUN FACT

The East, West and North Ridings come from the Viking word Thrithing, meaning a third part.

The 1200-year-old Coppergate helmet was found at York in 1982.

How do we know?

Most of our information about the Vikings comes from archaeological digs at York. In 1976, an old sweet factory was demolished in Coppergate. Lying beneath the ruins was an ancient Viking street with remains of buildings where Viking craftsmen had made spoons, cups and bowls. Archaeologists also found jewellery, leather, pottery, animal bones and much more, all preserved in the soil. Much of it is on display at Jorvik Viking Centre in York, giving us an incredible insight into Viking life. In 2007, a huge find of Viking gold and silver coins, jewellery and ingots was found in a field just outside Harrogate. This is known as the Vale of York Hoard and much of it is now displayed in the Yorkshire Museum.

Over 600 Yorkshire towns and villages still have Viking names. Check the Viking Place Names list above to see whether you live in one.

> First the Vikings came to raid, then to trade, then they stayed.

Feeding an Army

Katie hopes her freshly baked loaves will be enough to feed the hungry soldiers during their march south. King Harold's army looks tired. Defeating King Hardrada's horde of Vikings has taken much out of them, yet now they must turn and head for Hastings to face the French Duke of Normandy and his army. She wishes them luck.

King William said on his deathbed: 'I am stained with the rivers of blood that I have shed.'

Harrying of the North

New invaders from Normandy led by William, Duke of Normandy, defeated King Harold's tired army at the Battle of Hastings. William became King of England and later became known as William the Conqueror. Together with his victorious French knights, William swept to power across the whole of England. But he didn't always have it easy. Yorkshire folk revolted several times, throwing William's men out of York in 1067 and 1068.

William finally grew tired of the northern revolts and, during the winter of 1069-1070, began a cruel campaign. His army burned villages to the ground. Over 100,000 people were murdered. Farmland was burned, then salted, to stop crops growing for years to come. William's brutal campaign became known as the Harrying of the North.

SPOT THIS!

Can you spot the new Pontefract Market Hall which stands in the medieval market square?

Castles

William gave away the estates belonging to the Anglo-Saxon knights and barons to 28 of his closest friends; Norman lords with French names like Roger de Poitou, William de Percy, Roger de Busli and Ralph de Mortimer. They put the surviving local peasants to work building massive castles. Skipton Castle was built in 1090 by Roger de Romille. William de Warenne constructed Conisbrough Castle, Alain le Roux de Penthievre built his castle in Richmond, and Ilbert de Lacy erected his castle in Pontefract.

Skipton Castle has stood for over 900 years.

Fountains Abbey

After a disagreement at St Mary's Abbey, York in 1132, there was a riot. Thirteen monks were expelled, and set up Fountains Abbey. By the time Henry VIII seized Fountains Abbey in 1539, it was one of the richest monasteries in England.

FUN FACT
Symptoms of the plague included vomiting, headache, a furry tongue, swelling under the arm pits, black bruising and death!

Cheer up! You might be remembered at the Hepworth Feast along with plague victims from 1665.

Market Towns

The Norman lords rented out land on their estates and introduced weekly markets where traders came to sell cloth and other wares. Pontefract was granted its first market charter in 1194 and Wakefield's royal charter was granted in 1204. A charter for Scarborough Fair was granted by Henry III in 1253. It began on 15th August and lasted 45 days. Traders came from all over England and Europe.

The lords of the manor had enormous power to raise taxes and to sentence criminals. The Lord of Wakefield Manor had the power to send prisoners to hang from the gibbet.

Pestilence

By the 1300s, Yorkshire had recovered from the Harrying when disaster struck. Bad weather caused crops to fail and animals to perish. And to make matters worse, in the spring of 1349 the Black Death plague arrived, wiping out almost one third of Yorkshire's population.

| CELT 500 BC | ROMAN AD 43–410 | ANGLO-SAXON AD 450–1066 | VIKING AD 865–1066 | MEDIEVAL TIMES 1066–148 |

Hilda is 10 years old. She lives in a farming village near Pontefract. Here is an imaginary message from Hilda to her uncle living in the south, pleading for help.

100,000 people from the north died as a result of the Harrying of the North.

FUN FACT
Punishment for stealing a 'piece' of cloth was execution on the lethal Halifax Gibbet, an early type of guillotine.

Winter, 1069

Dear Uncle,
Please help me. Norman soldiers have attacked our village and my father and many of our neighbours are dead! The soldiers arrived on horseback and set fire to the thatch roofs. Our house was the first to burn and when Father tried to stop the soldiers killing our animals, he was cut down by a sword. I became separated from Mother and my little brother Tordic, and I haven't seen them since.
With a few survivors, I escaped to the moors where we hid amongst the peat bogs until the soldiers had gone. I could see for miles up there, all the way to Jorvik and the land was scorched. Everywhere was on fire. No village or settlement has survived.
Some days later, we tried returning to the village but packs of dogs and wolves drove us away. I have no food. There are no crops in the ground, the summer harvest has been burned - we are slowly starving.
Your loving niece, Hilda

14

"Are you going to Scarborough Fair? Parsley, sage rosemary and thyme. Remember me to one who lives there. She once was a true love of mine."

Do you know the tune to this old English ballad?

The ruins of Fountains Abbey

How do we know?

Much of what we know about the Harrying of the North comes from medieval chronicles. Orderic Vitalis recorded the events of the day in the *Historia Ecclesiastica*. A later writer, Symeon of Durham, reported that, between York and Durham, no village was inhabited, and that for nine years, the area was deserted except by bandits and wild animals. Even the Doomsday Book, commissioned by William the Conqueror in 1085, records the Harrying. Many entries for Yorkshire villages read 'now it is waste' seventeen years after the event. Indeed, the records show that 480 Yorkshire towns and villages were 'wholly wasted' and another 314 'partly wasted'. These were harsh times, when even a petty thief could end up losing his head on the Halifax gibbet.

Medieval Yorkshire suffered famine, plague and fire on a grand scale.

To Battle!

Joshua is frightened by all the talk of Civil War. Around him, friends and family are choosing sides. Soon he will make his choice, then face the boom of cannon and the acrid smell of spent gunpowder as the country goes to war.

> The Tudor rose combines the red rose of Lancaster and the white rose of York!

Wars of the Roses

The Wars of the Roses were a series of battles between two rival claims to the English throne, those of the House of York and the House of Lancaster.

Yorkshire had supporters of both Houses. The East and West Ridings mainly supported Lancaster, whose symbol was the red rose. The North Riding was loyal to York, whose symbol was the white rose.

The wars lasted thirty years, from 1455 to 1485, and the fiercest battles were in Yorkshire. The Battle of Towton, on 29th March 1461, is said to be the bloodiest ever – 20,000 men died that day. The Battle of Wakefield, in 1460, was so fierce that the nearby beck ran red with the blood of the fallen. Eventually, Lancaster was victorious and Henry Tudor claimed the throne.

Damaged skulls from the Battle of Wakefield

Gunpowder Plot

In the 1600s, Catholic rebels planned to murder the Protestant King James I during the official opening of Parliament, 5th November 1605. This group included a Yorkshire man, called Guy Fawkes, who planned to use gunpowder to blow up the Houses of Parliament. This 'Gunpowder Plot' was foiled when Fawkes was arrested at midnight on 4th November and his barrels of gunpowder were discovered. Having foiled the plot, King James proclaimed the 5th of November to be a Day of Thanksgiving and asked that bonfires be lit in celebration. Bonfire Night has become a tradition.

Pontefract Castle was destroyed after the Civil War.

Civil War

The English Civil War began in 1642 between the Roundheads who supported Parliament and the Cavaliers who supported King Charles I. The people of Yorkshire were split: the Cavaliers made York their base and the Roundheads settled in Hull. The two sides fought at the Battle of Adwalton Moor, which the Royalists won, and later at the Battle of Marston Moor, when the Roundheads were victorious.

Led by Oliver Cromwell, the Roundheads triumphed and the king was executed in 1649. After the war, Parliament ordered that all castles used by the Royalists should be destroyed. Castles in Pontefract, Sheffield, Knaresborough, Sandal and many more were left in ruins.

FUN FACT
When King Charles I came looking for weapons in Hull in 1642, he was refused entry to the city and driven away by angry Parliamentarians.

The people of Yorkshire were divided by the Civil War.

SPOT THIS!
Can you spot the Battle of Towton memorial near Tadcaster?

Machines and Mills

It's six o'clock in the morning when sisters Hatty and Flo walk through the iron gates of a large cloth mill. They work with over three hundred other people in a huge machine room filled with dust and noise. Their 14-hour shift won't end until eight o'clock this evening.

Thomas Boulsover of Sheffield

SPOT THIS!

Spot this at Halifax Piece Hall, built in 1779, where farmers sold their 'pieces' of cloth.

Steel

With the Civil War over, towns like Sheffield, Doncaster, Halifax and Bradford began to prosper.

In the 1740s, Benjamin Huntsman invented Crucible Steel and set up in Attercliffe. According to legend, a Sheffield rival called Samuel Walker dressed up as a beggar and asked if he could shelter in one of Huntsman's factories. While he pretended to sleep, Walker worked out Huntsman's steel-making method and stole it for himself.

In 1743, a cutler named Thomas Boulsover accidentally combined silver with copper to invent Sheffield Plate. His product resembled solid silver but was cheaper to produce, and he quickly made his fortune making buttons. By now Sheffield had also overtaken London as Britain's cutlery centre, manufacturing most of the world's cutlery.

...1742 CRUCIBLE STEEL INVENTED...1774 LEEDS LIVERPOOL CANAL OPENS...

Kersey Cloth

In Halifax and Calderdale, local farmers and their families were spinning yarn from wool fleeces and weaving individual 'pieces' of Kersey cloth. The pieces were made on a hand loom and sold to merchants in huge cloth halls. Halifax soon became one of England's most important and wealthy cloth-making centres.

Then, in 1785, Doncaster man Edmund Cartwright invented the power loom. This machine could weave better quality cloth at a faster rate than a hand loom. More and more mill owners began to use power looms so that, soon, fewer skilled weavers were needed. This was the beginning of the Industrial Revolution.

Leeds and Liverpool Canal near Saltaire.

Ee baaa gum! Swaledale wool's t'best.

The Leeds and Liverpool Canal was built to carry woollen cloth in 1773.

FUN FACT
Families made a piece of Kersey cloth 30 yards (27.5 metres) long, for sale at the weekly market, on a handloom.

Worstedopolis

Bradford's reputation for producing fine worsted cloth led to the city's nickname – Worstedopolis. Factories and mills were springing up everywhere, each driven by great steam-powered machines and looms. Soon, people flocked to what had once been a small market town, looking for jobs. Bradford couldn't cope. Its streets and tiny back-to-back homes became overcrowded and filthy. Sewage leaked into Bradford canal so locals nicknamed it River Stink.

Luddites

A group called the Luddites – named after a fictional rebel Captain Ludd – feared the new machines would leave skilled men out of work and began destroying machinery and burning mills. The movement became so strong that they even clashed with the British Army. Eventually, the government brought many Luddites to trial in York, where three men were found guilty and executed, and seven others were transported to Australia.

Hatty and Flo live in Huddersfield and work in a woollen mill. They make fine cloth in navy blue and black which is used to make army and navy uniforms. This imaginary letter is from Hatty.

Since I started work at the mill, I can't stop coughing at night.

Sunday, 14th December, 1834

Dear Auntie,

Father has sold the sheep and our spinning wheel as we can't make enough money spinning and weaving pieces any more. The big mills are making cloth so much faster!

We used to make a piece of cloth thirty yards long in just a week. Our kersey was good quality too. Father could always sell them for a good price at Ramsden's Cloth Hall on Saturday mornings. Not any more!

Flo and I have got ourselves jobs in the mill working on the power looms. The machines are so noisy! When we come out our ears are ringing from the knock-knock-knock of the loom. It's very dusty and greasy too, so our clothes are really grimy when we finish our long shift.

Flo and I are saving every spare penny to buy new aprons and caps and perhaps some new leather clogs! We're going to save them for Sunday best and only wear them to church. Flo has a boy that's sweet on her and has asked her to walk out with him after the church service!

Give our love to our cousins. We miss them!

Love Hatty

Workers' back-to-back homes.

FUN FACT
Benjamin Law of Batley used leftover wool to produce cheap cloth called Shoddy.

20

Yorkshire Penny

Pontefract is one of the only places in Britain where liquorice grows. When a chemist named George Dunhill added sugar to liquorice in 1760, a sweet called the 'Yorkshire Penny' was invented, which we now know as the Pontefract Cake.

JOSHUA TETLEY (1778–1859)
In 1822 Joshua Tetley bought William Sykes' brewery business which had stood here since 1792. Joshua's enterprise and fine quality ales created a reputation which for over 150 years has made the name 'Tetleys' synonymous with the City of Leeds.

William Wilberforce was a small man with a big ambition: to abolish the slave trade.

Drinking water was often dirty, so beer was important.

Yorkshire's mills and mines made a few families wealthy but kept most people poor.

How do we know?

Records show that Kersey cloth from Halifax made up a third of the country's textile output. Napoleon's armies were said to have worn uniforms made from fabric produced in Yorkshire. Records of price lists show that much of the cheapest Shoddy cloth was sold to the American colonies as slave clothes and blankets. The Health of Towns Commissioners described Bradford as 'the dirtiest, filthiest and worst town in the kingdom...' Even the preacher John Wesley took one look at Huddersfield and said: 'A wilder people I never saw in England...' Speeches made by William Wilberforce, MP for Kingston upon Hull, in the House of Commons tell us about social reforms he helped bring about, including ending the slave trade.

Rail Mania!

Ruth stares up at the huge machine. Clouds of steam billow from its chimney, the smell of burning coal tickles her nostrils and her ears buzz with a loud 'toot' each time the driver pulls its whistle. But what excites Ruth the most is the journey ahead of her – by steam train from Doncaster to Scarborough and her first ever seaside holiday!

The Grand Hotel, Scarborough in the 1890s.

Railway Mania

By the mid 1840s, railways began taking over from slower canal transport. Woodhead Tunnel, on the line from Manchester to Sheffield, was one of the longest in the world at almost 5 kilometres. It took six years to complete and employed over 1,500 navvies. Thirty-two men died during the build.

The Doncaster Railway Works turned Doncaster into a bustling town by 1891, producing almost 100 locomotives each year. These powerful engines hauled heavy steam trains including the most famous ever, The Flying Scotsman.

The railways began a new fashion for ordinary Yorkshire families, who could now visit the seaside at Scarborough. Sea bathing became so popular that Scarborough soon became the most visited Victorian holiday resort. The Grand Hotel, built in 1867, had 12 floors, 52 chimneys and 365 bedrooms. It was one of the biggest hotels in the world.

FUN FACT
Children didn't just work in the mills, they slept in them too.

Black Gold

Coal, or Black Gold, had always been mined in Yorkshire and as industry grew, so did its demand for coal. Most mines were small. Lawwood was owned by the 4th Earl Fitzwilliam and employed only 19 'picks' or miners. However, larger collieries soon opened, the first of which was in Middleton, employing over 150 people by the early 1800s.

Giant cloth mills sprang up all over Yorkshire. John Marshall built vast mills in Adel and Holbeck. Benjamin Gotts, another Leeds mill owner, employed over 12,000 people as Leeds soon overtook Halifax as the region's centre for cloth production.

SPOT THIS!

You can see what life was like down a mine at the National Coal Mining Museum, Wakefield.

Joseph Rowntree, the sweet-maker, set up trust funds that still help people today.

Akroyd's model village, Akroydon, built in the 1850s.

All Work, No Play

The sudden growth of cities like Leeds and Bradford left many workers living in overcrowded houses. Diseases spread quickly in these places. When cholera broke out in Leeds in 1832, half of all those who died were under the age of five.

Poor children didn't go to school. Instead, they worked in mills and factories from six o'clock in the morning until eight o'clock at night. Many suffered from bent and crippled legs caused by standing for long periods and poor diets. An Act of Parliament was passed in 1833, forbidding mills to employ children under nine years of age. Those aged between 9 and 14 could work no more than twelve hours a day, and only nine hours on Saturday.

Model Village

Eventually, the wealthy mill and factory owners realised that they would have to provide their workers with better living and working conditions. 'Model' villages were built by Titus Salt in Saltaire and Edward Akroyd in Calderdale. They provided comfortable houses, schools and churches for their workers. Akroyd also founded the Yorkshire Penny Bank, now known as Yorkshire Bank, to encourage his workers to save.

Billy is a 10-year-old lad who lives just outside the village of Middleton. This imaginary account describes his first day at the Colliery.

> I go to work when it's still dark, I work in the dark, then come home when it's getting dark!

Monday 5 March, 1838

Today I took myself off to the colliery at Middleton in Leeds and got work as a Hurrier. I was a bit scared being lowered down that deep, dark mine shaft the first time, but I didn't show it!

The men hack great chunks of coal out of a seam in the rock and load it into small carts called corfs. When the corf is full, it's my job to drag or 'hurry' it up to the surface.

I've got to be quick because we're all paid by how much coal we produce, so the more 'hurries' I can make in a shift, the better. And I reckon I could do more than twenty 'hurries' in every twelve hour shift, I'll tell thee.

The foreman said I was just the right size; being small I can bend to fit inside the tunnel. I've got two five-year-olds helping me. They're working as thrusters and their job is to help push the cart, with their heads – one of them has been working there for six months and the hair on his crown has worn away!

At the end of my first day, it was getting dark when I came up from the pit, but it still seemed bright to my eyes. I wish I'd been here when John Blenkinsop was in charge at Middleton. Folk say he was a genius for inventing a railway that can haul coal trucks twice as heavy as at other collieries. Maybe he could have invented something to make my job easier!

The 'Flying Scotsman' was built at Doncaster Works.

FUN FACT
Bram Stoker wrote 'Dracula' after a ship carrying coffins sank off Whitby and the coffins were washed up on the shore.

Sporting Yorkshire

By the mid 1800s, Victorians realised the importance of fresh air and exercise. New parks were built for people to escape to smog of the town and to enjoy sports. In 1863, the Yorkshire County Cricket Club was founded. The Yorkshire Cup began in 1878 when Halifax beat York to win 'T'owd Tin Pot'. Huddersfield became the birthplace of rugby league in 1895 when some northern clubs broke away from the Rugby Football Union.

The first rack railway introduced by John Blenkinsop in 1812.

How do we know?

In 1841, Parliament commissioned a report into child labour in the mining industry. Their findings made grim reading. One witness, Benjamin Mellow, a superintendent at Silkstone, recalled a disaster at the colliery in 1838 in which 26 children died. The Commission's report led to the 1842 Act of Parliament, banning the employment of women, and boys under the age of 10 years.

Richard Oastler from Leeds led a campaign for a 10-hour working day in factories which resulted in the 'Ten Hour Act' in 1847.

Yorkshire workers' living and working conditions began to improve.

COLLIERY Disaster

On 4th July 1838, disaster struck the small mining village of Silkstone near Barnsley. In what is being called the Huskar Pit Disaster, a freak storm flooded part of the mine, killing 26 children.

25

Evacuate!

The cottage is small and a long way from Hull. The people seem nice, but Colin can tell they'd rather not have a couple of 'evacuees' from the city in their home. Outside, the smell of burning buildings has been replaced by fresh country air. And local people gaze towards the sky in search of birds or clouds, not to spot German planes and bombs.

Queen Victoria Square in Hull during the Blitz.

FUN FACT
Clothes and food were in short supply during the war so people were given ration books to make sure that everyone had a fair share.

World War Two

In World War Two, Yorkshire's large industrial towns were major targets, with Sheffield and Hull being badly bombed. The worst bombing raids were over Hull between 13th and 18th March 1941 and, by the end of the war, over 5,000 houses, 27 churches and 14 schools and hospitals had all been destroyed.

Many of the school-age children were 'evacuated'. This meant that children from towns like Leeds and Bradford were sent to stay in quieter, safer towns such as Ilkley, Otley, Wetherby and Harrogate, where they were taken in by locals until the war had ended.

After the War

After the war, men came back from fighting and took back their old jobs in the mining, steel and textile industries. In the 1950s, times were good. However, in the 1960s and 1970s cheaper foreign competition led to many old-established steel and textile firms closing or reducing in size. Hull's fishing trade suffered a blow when the trawlers were no longer allowed to fish for cod off the shores of Iceland.

Miners' Strike

In the 1980s, cheap coal was imported from abroad. When the government announced that it was to close unprofitable coal mines, starting with Cortonwood Colliery, the miners' unions called a national strike which lasted almost a year. The coal miners weren't successful and many of their mines were eventually closed. In 1984, before the strike, Britain had 174 coal mines. Today, only six remain.

SPOT THIS!

The Kilburn White Horse on the North York Moors was covered up during World War Two so that German bombers couldn't use it to navigate by.

COAL NOT DOLE

'Dole' is another word for welfare benefits.

Today, Yorkshire is famous for sport, television and tourism.

How do we know?

We are lucky to have people alive today who were evacuated as children and can tell us what it was like for them. Photographs from the time and newsreel films shown in cinemas give us an idea of what life was like in wartime. But these were often made to lift people's spirits and didn't show the worst things that were happening. Newspapers, posters and leaflets also give us information about wartime Yorkshire. Films and TV documentaries record the lives of people during the Miners' Strike and what happened to the villages after the pits closed.

Today and Tomorrow

Yorkshire has come a long way since the Romans arrived 2,000 years ago. We know how it has changed thanks to objects dug from the ground, written records, old maps and paintings and the many historical buildings that survive. So how will people know about today's Yorkshire folk in the future?

← Yorkshire's known for its puddings, liquorice and Betty's Tearooms. Will they still be enjoyed in 100 years?

↑ From back-to-back homes to Bridgewater Place, Yorkshire's tallest skyscraper, what kind of homes will we have in future?

You can feel proud to belong to Yorkshire – 'God's Own Country'!

← See modern sculptures by Henry Moore and Barbara Hepworth, old paintings from the Gott Collection and more at the Hepworth Wakefield gallery.

...1953 Tetley teabag launched...1972 Leeds United win FA Cup...

FUN FACT
The Rhubarb Triangle, between Wakefield, Morley and Rothwell, grows 90% of the world's forced winter rhubarb!

⬆ Fred Truman, Geoffrey Boycott, Kevin Keegan, Jessica Ennis – just a few famous Yorkshire sports names. With the English Institute of Sport in Sheffield, there are sure to be plenty in future.

⬆ Howarth Parsonage Museum records the lives of the Bronte sisters. Many famous writers, including the Bronte sisters, Arthur Ransome, James Herriot and Alan Bennett have come from Yorkshire. Who will be the next?

⬅ The great explorer, Captain James Cook, was born in Marton, Middlesbrough.

⬆ There has been a lighthouse at Flamborough Head since the 1600s. Will it still be there in another 400 years?

How will they know?

How will future generations know what Yorkshire was like for us, now? The internet is a great way of recording the present. Photos, blogs and stories from tourists can all spread the word about our wonderful coastline, dales and the moors. Hundreds of years from now someone may be looking at your picture or reading your blog. You're making history!

Glossary

Abbey – a building where monks or nuns live and work. An Abbot is in charge of monks, an Abbess is in charge of nuns.

AD – a short way to write anno Domini, which is Latin and means 'in the year of Our Lord', i.e. after the birth of Christ.

Air raid – during World War Two, enemy planes dropped bombs on Britain. This was an air raid. To warn people the planes were coming, sirens wailed out all over the city and everyone hid in air raid shelters.

Archaeologist – a person who studies the past by examining buildings and objects left behind by previous people and cultures.

Back-to-backs – houses built so closely together they had only a small space between them.

Barracks – a building where soldiers stay.

Blitz – Bombing raids over British cities by the Germans during World War Two.

Catholic – a member of the Christian religion that considers the Pope its head.

Centurion – an officer in the Roman army, originally in charge of 80 soldiers.

Charter – written permission to do something. A royal charter means the king or queen has given permission.

Cholera – a deadly disease caused by filthy water.

Civil war – a war where people in the same country fight each other.

Domesday Book – a record, ordered by William the Conqueror, of property, land, people and animals in 11th-century Britain.

Evacuee – a person who has to leave their home because it is no longer safe.

Excavation – a site where people dig, often archaeologists looking for buried objects to find out about the past.

Famine – a shortage of food so bad that people starve to death.

Fleece – the coat that covers a sheep. People can wear the wool or weave it to make cloth.

Gibbet – a scaffold post where executed criminals were left to hang as a warning to others.

Hadrian's Wall – a wall built by the Roman Emperor Hadrian across Northern Britain to keep out the northern tribes. Some of the wall still survives.

Monastery – a place where monks live and worship.

Monk – a male member of a religious community that has rules of poverty, chastity and obedience.

Parliamentarian – anyone who fought on the side of Oliver Cromwell and Parliament in the English Civil War. Also known as a Roundhead.

Protestant – a member of the Christian religion that considers the king or queen of England to be the head of its church.

Province – a territory governed by a country. The Romans divided the land they conquered into provinces.

Ration book – during World War Two, certain foods were scarce. Your Ration Book showed how much of this food you could have every week.

Sewer – underground pipes where all waste matter goes.

Slave trade – making money by buying and selling people as slaves. Slaves have no freedom or rights and work for nothing.

Vicus – Roman name for a town that grew up outside a fort.

Index

Acknowledgements

The publishers would like to thank the following people and organizations
for their permission to reproduce material on the following pages:

Cover: CaptureLight/Shutterstock; ronfromyork/Shutterstock
p5: Alan Rosevear/Flickr; p7: © West Yorkshire Archaeology Advisory Service, reproduced by permission, Copyright © Archaeological Services WYAS, image courtesy of Wakefield Council;p9: Rod Mackey/Wikipedia; p11: York Archaeological Trust, www.jorvik-viking-centre.co.uk; p12: Andrew Stopford/Flickr; p13: Christina Bollen/Alamy; p15: CJ08/Shutterstock; p16: Copyright © Wakefield Council; p17: Thomas Ackroyd/Flickr; p18: pdtnc/Shutterstock; p20: Mary Evans Picture Library; p22: Mary Evans Picture Library; p23: Traveland Landscape UK/Mark Sykes/Alamy, Tim Green/Flickr; p24: Rich@rd/Wikipedia; p25: By kind permission of Leeds Library and Information Services, www.leodis.net; p26: Hull History Centre; p27: Alan Curtis/Alamy; p28: Geraldine Curtis/Flickr; p29: English Institute of Sport, Eric James/Alamy, Allstar Picture Library / Alamy
All other images copyright of Hometown World

Written by Andrew Newbound
Educational consultant: Neil Thompson
Local history consultant: Allison Freeman
Designed by Sarah Allen

Illustrated by Kate Davies, Dynamo Ltd, Virginia Gray, Tim Hutchinson,
Peter Kent, Nick Shewring and Tim Sutcliffe
Additional photographs by Alex Long

First published by HOMETOWN WORLD in 2012
Hometown World Ltd
7 Northumberland Buildings
Bath BA1 2JB

www.hometownworld.co.uk

ISBN 978-1-84993-209-7

BYE!

CELT
500 BC

ROMAN
AD 43–410

ANGLO-SAXON
AD 450–1066

VIKING
AD 865–1066

MEDIEVAL TIMES
1066–1485